Fourth Workshop on Privacy in Natural Language Processing (PrivateNLP 2022)

Online
15 June 2022

ISBN: 978-1-7138-5636-8

Printed from e-media with permission by:

Curran Associates, Inc.
57 Morehouse Lane
Red Hook, NY 12571

Some format issues inherent in the e-media version may also appear in this print version.

Printed with permission by Curran Associates, Inc. (2022)

For permission requests, please contact the Association for Computational Linguistics at the address below.

Association for Computational Linguistics
209 N. Eighth Street
Stroudsburg, Pennsylvania 18360

Phone: 1-570-476-8006
Fax: 1-570-476-0860

acl@aclweb.org

Additional copies of this publication are available from:

Curran Associates, Inc.
57 Morehouse Lane
Red Hook, NY 12571 USA
Phone: 845-758-0400
Fax: 845-758-2633
Email: curran@proceedings.com
Web: www.proceedings.com

PrivateNLP 2022

The 2022 Conference of the North American Chapter of the Association for Computational Linguistics: Human Language Technologies

Proceedings of the Workshop

July 15, 2022

Order copies of this and other ACL proceedings from:

Association for Computational Linguistics (ACL)
209 N. Eighth Street
Stroudsburg, PA 18360
USA
Tel: +1-570-476-8006
Fax: +1-570-476-0860
acl@aclweb.org

Organizing Committee

Workshop Organizers

Oluwaseyi Feyisetan, Meta, USA
Sepideh Ghanavati, University of Maine, USA
Patricia Thaine, University of Toronto, Canada
Ivan Habernal, Technische Universität Darmstadt, Germany
Fatemehsadat Mireshghallah, University of California, San Diego

Program Committee

Past and Current Program Committee

Andreas Nautsch, EUROCOM
Abhinav Aggarwal, Amazon
Asma Aloufi, Rochester Institute of Technology
Balazs Pejo, Budapest University of Technology and Economics
Benjamin Zi Hao Zhao, University of New South Wales
Borja Balle, Deepmind
Briland Hitaj, SRI International
Christian Weinert, Technische Universitat Darmstadt
Congzheng Song, Apple
Dinusha Vatsalan, Data61-CSIRO
Eleftheria Makri, Saxion University
Elette Boyle, IDC Herzliya
Isar Nejadgholi, National Research Council Canada
Jamie Hayes, University College London
Jason Xue, University of Adelaide
Kambiz Ghazinour, State University of New York
Ken Barker, University of Calgary
Liwei Song, Princeton
Luca Melis, Meta
Mitra Bokaei Hosseini, St Marys University
Natasha Fernandes, Macquarie University
Nedelina Teneva, Amazon
Peizhao Hu, Rochester Institute of Technology
Sai Di Teja Peddinti, Google
Sanonda Datta, University of Maine
Sebastian Walter, Semalytix
Shomir Wilson, Pennsylvania State University
Tom Diethe, Amazon
Travis Breaux, Carnegie Mellon University
Vijayanta Jaine, University of Maine
Xavier Ferrer, Kings College London
Zekun Xu, Amazon

Invited Speakers

Ilya Mironov, Meta, USA
Franziska Boenisch, Fraunhofer AISEC
Esha Ghosh, Microsoft

Table of Contents

Differential Privacy in Natural Language Processing: The Story So Far

Oleksandra Klymenko, Stephen Meisenbacher and **Florian Matthes**
Technical University of Munich
Department of Informatics
Garching, Germany
{alexandra.klymenko, stephen.meisenbacher, matthes}@tum.de

Abstract

As the tide of Big Data continues to influence the landscape of Natural Language Processing (NLP), the utilization of modern NLP methods has grounded itself in this data, in order to tackle a variety of text-based tasks. These methods without a doubt can include private or otherwise personally identifiable information. As such, the question of privacy in NLP has gained fervor in recent years, coinciding with the development of new Privacy-Enhancing Technologies (PETs). Among these PETs, Differential Privacy boasts several desirable qualities in the conversation surrounding data privacy. Naturally, the question becomes whether Differential Privacy is applicable in the largely unstructured realm of NLP. This topic has sparked novel research, which is unified in one basic goal: how can one adapt Differential Privacy to NLP methods? This paper aims to summarize the vulnerabilities addressed by Differential Privacy, the current thinking, and above all, the crucial next steps that must be considered.

1 Introduction

In an age where a vast amount of data is being produced daily, the opportunities created by this proliferation increase concurrently. The availability of big data enables countless downstream tasks whose accuracy and utility seem to increase with the amount of data used. Specifically, the fields of Machine Learning (ML) and Deep Learning (DL) have profited from such data. Particularly in the case of Natural Language Processing (NLP), the tasks at hand more often than not concern the handling of *unstructured* data, meaning data that is not neatly organized into a traditional row-like database structure, and furthermore, data that is not necessarily static. In fact, it is estimated that data on the order of zettabytes (ZB) is being produced every day (Begum and Nausheen, 2018), and within this amount, roughly 80% is unstructured, e.g. textual data (Hammoud et al., 2019).

At the same time as this profound boom in popularity of big data tasks, there has been an increase in the attention paid to the way in which data is used, specifically to the issue of *privacy*. The problem is exacerbated when sensitive parts of the data relate to a specific task (e.g. with medical data). The threat becomes more serious when the models themselves used with the learning tasks are vulnerable to attacks.

Although many useful Privacy-Enhancing Technologies have emerged, one in particular seems to be a good fit when faced with the scale of these big data learning tasks: Differential Privacy (Dwork, 2006). The key feature of Differential Privacy is its mathematically grounded notion of privacy, which can be intuitively explained using the privacy parameter, most often called ϵ. This idea was originally intended for data stored in structured databases, i.e. a relational schema. As a result, Differential Privacy upon its inception became an excellent way to start to reason about privacy in ML and DL models that were trained on these types of databases.

Alas, in the field of NLP, where the core unit of data is unstructured, fuzzy text rather than a structured data point, an initial attempt to apply Differential Privacy poses some challenges. Chief among these is the challenge of how to transfer the core concepts of Differential Privacy, namely the "individual" and *adjacency*, to the textual domain where these concepts are not easily perceivable. Thus, it becomes the goal to find new ways of reasoning about Differential Privacy in order to adapt it to the unstructured data domain of NLP. Through the course of this paper, the foundations of Differential Privacy in the lens of NLP will be investigated, motivated by some privacy vulnerabilities that surface from NLP techniques. Afterwards, the limitations and open questions of Differential Privacy with NLP will be analyzed with an in-depth discussion.

Proceedings of the Fourth Workshop on Privacy in Natural Language Processing, pages 1 - 11
July 15, 2022

2 Foundations

Privacy-Enhancing Technologies Several PETs have been created with the goal of protecting the privacy of the individuals. Three methods in particular have arisen as useful ways to reason about groups in a dataset: *k-anonymity* (Samarati and Sweeney, 1998), *l-diversity* (Machanavajjhala et al., 2007), and *t-closeness* (Li et al., 2007). These frameworks are quite reliant upon the structured nature of a database, yet they become impractical in the realm of large-scale, unstructured data. They therefore lack a reasonable applicability to NLP. Addressing privacy concerns within text, traditional methods include simple redaction or scrubbing based upon available heuristics. Newer notions, such as *t-plausibility* (Jiang et al., 2009), were designed with text document sanitization in mind. Finally, modern approaches involve the idea of *adversarial learning*, such as (Elazar and Goldberg, 2018) or (Friedrich et al., 2019). As one may postulate, Differential Privacy also lacks a direct mapping to NLP, becoming the basis of investigation in the pursuit of differentially private NLP.

Differential Privacy in ML and DL Researchers first looked to determine the place of Differential Privacy in ML and DL. The following papers on Differential Privacy in ML (Ji et al., 2014) and DL (Abadi et al., 2016) are great starting points for applying Differential Privacy to these areas. Importantly, it has been shown that Differential Privacy does indeed have a place when considering these types of learning tasks. Not until later was the idea extended to NLP, and even today, the research on it is still relatively scarce. This is due precisely to some of the reasons introduced in Section 1. Nevertheless, this extra layer of complexity makes Differential Privacy in NLP an interesting topic. There exist papers that systematize this topic for ML, such as (Al-Rubaie and Chang, 2019), and DL (Boulemtafes et al., 2019), which partially cover Differential Privacy, but to the best of the authors' knowledge, no such papers specifically address its application to NLP. Thus, it becomes the goal to start to bridge this gap.

3 Methodology

To accomplish the goals of this paper, the following research questions have been defined:

RQ1 What vulnerabilities to NLP techniques is Differential Privacy capable of preventing?

RQ2 What is the current state of Differential Privacy in its application to NLP?

RQ3 What are the predominant current limitations and future directions of applying Differential Privacy to NLP?

The structure of the research supporting this paper is twofold, firstly taking the form of a systematic literature review. Thus, the main method of answering the stated research questions will be to seek out relevant academic literature and research, which will serve as the primary source for data synthesis. This process, including formulating a search process and creating exclusion criteria, is based upon Garousi (Garousi et al., 2019).

The second stage of research involves conducting semi-structured expert interviews. The main goal of these is to supplement the knowledge gained from the literature with practical viewpoints from privacy professionals and relevant academic researchers. This is crucial to harmonizing the promise of research with the demands of industry, and ultimately, society. Table 1 shows a summary of the four interviews conducted. The insights from these interviews will be highlighted in the discussion conducted in Section 7.

Code	Position	Organization
I1	Co-Founder and CEO	Privacy-focused AI startup, Canada
I2	Postdoctoral Research Associate	University, Australia
I3	Applied Science Manager	Research division of large American tech company
I4	PhD Candidate	University, USA

Table 1: Coded Interviewee Table

The remainder of this paper is structured as follows: Section 4 begins our exploration of Differential Privacy in NLP by first analyzing which privacy vulnerabilities Differential Privacy is best suited to address (RQ1). Next, Section 5 introduces Differential Privacy in the scope of how it has been adapted to textual data (RQ2). Section 6 continues this narrative by focusing on a generalization of Differential Privacy that is well-suited for unstructured domains (RQ2). Finally, Section 7 comprises of several discussion points that are seen to be pertinent current limitations, and accordingly, crucial future research directions (RQ3).

4 Privacy Vulnerabilities in NLP Techniques

By first analyzing some privacy vulnerabilities in NLP techniques (RQ1), we hope to motivate the thinking behind the incorporation of Differential Privacy in NLP, presented in Sections 5 and 6. Here, we differentiate between two overarching categories of vulnerabilties: (1) *information leakage* (Song and Raghunathan, 2020) and (2) *unintended memorization* (Carlini et al., 2019). The focus is placed on the former, as this is more relevant to NLP, while the latter pertains more generally to the DL applications.

4.1 Language Leakage

When approaching any number of NLP tasks, the first step ultimately becomes finding an appropriate text representation. An early, simple example of this would be the Bag-of-Words model, or representing text by a set of linguistic-based features. This kind of modeling, however, also enables the building of a "stylometric profile". In the wrong hands, the collection of these features can give up *implicit information*, which is not explicitly sensitive but can highlight user (author) attributes. This type of hidden information is known as *information leakage*, but in light of the focus on textual data, we use the term *language leakage*. Such a generalization aids in seeing that both traditional and more modern (i.e. embedding) representations of text are susceptible to such leakage.

In recent years, the growing success of word embeddings for use as general purpose language models has rooted their utilization in downstream tasks. The usefulness of these models lies in the fact that numerical representations of textual data can be used for computation in a wide variety of learning tasks, where plaintext does not readily fit. Also inherent to these models are useful properties that can capture word associations. In order to create them, word embeddings are usually trained on vast amounts of text. These texts could contain private or sensitive information, which in turn are encoded into the vector representations. This poses a problem with embeddings, whose goal is to capture semantic meaning of words, without an inherent concept of private information.

Beyond embeddings, the rising ubiquity of (large) language models, or (L)LMs, such as GPT-2/3, has called to question Differential Privacy's role in this domain. For similar reasons as embeddings, LMs trained on massive amounts of textual data are susceptible to leakage of sensitive information contained therein. As such, it becomes the task to incorporate Differential Privacy into these LMs to defend against inference attacks, while still preserving their utility.

4.1.1 Exploitation

When thinking about the components of text that may comprise sensitive information, one may imagine that much of this follows a structured, fixed format. Examples of this include, but are not limited to, Social Security numbers (SSNs), birth dates, and phone numbers. When textual data contains such structure, it can become the goal of an attacker to recover, or reconstruct, these fixed-formatted strings. Such attacks have been shown to be effective by (Pan et al., 2020) and (Carlini et al., 2020), especially when certain embedding models are utilized. As such, exploiting language leakage within text representations generally revolves around *inference*.

Keyword inference attacks present a more general attack model, where the attacker has an idea of what kind of text is contained in the released data. Concretely, the attacker's goal is to extract keywords from the data, given some domain knowledge. It is shown in (Pan et al., 2020) that keyword extraction is also possible where the attacker has little to no domain knowledge of the data.

In addition to extracting information about input data in embedding models, the authors in (Song and Raghunathan, 2020) demonstrate the ability to extract author attributes. Furthermore, the structure of embedding models is susceptible to leaking membership information, especially with infrequently occurring inputs to the embedding model. Similar results concerning the inference of author attributes come out of (Coavoux et al., 2018).

Alarmingly, it has been shown that even a simple combination of lexical and syntactic features can be used to predict the gender of a text's author with approximately 80% accuracy (Koppel, 2002) - and this is done with a relatively simple, non-neural classifier. Other similar cases are covered in (Elazar and Goldberg, 2018). One might imagine how such features can not only expose author attributes, but also the author's identity.

4.2 Unintended Memorization

As the prevalence of neural NLP has been on the rise in recent years, concerns about the ability of neural networks to memorize data, or rather the patterns therein, has lead to questions of privacy breaches. In (Carlini et al., 2019), it is shown that a relatively rare-occurring *secret* in the training text can cause a neural model to memorize it completely. In some cases, such memorization seems to be a necessary part of the training process. The authors in (Thomas et al., 2020) show that certain word embedding models, when used in neural networks, lead to unintended memorization. Although solutions to this problem involve Differential Privacy (Abadi et al., 2016; Carlini et al., 2019; Yu et al., 2021b), it is not the main focus of this paper.

4.3 Risk Use Cases

We discuss two general categories of risk use cases Differential Privacy in NLP can address, as well as imply when it is not appropriate.

4.3.1 Data Release

Often, it might make sense to release (unstructured) textual data to third parties. In many of these cases, however, the text being released contains sensitive information. A well-studied example of this is the release of medical data, which can take the form of hospital records or doctors' notes (Li and Qin, 2018). Other prevalent use cases include the release of text from online reviews, social media posts, or government records (Pan et al., 2020), all of which can contain quite sensitive information. For data release, such data is often transferred to third parties in de-identified form (Abdalla et al., 2020b), with the thought that this inherently provides a first layer of defense. Even so, a malicious user with access can extract personal information, showcased in (Abdalla et al., 2020a), which shows that releasing medical data in embedding form still allows for nearly 70% reconstruction of Personally Identifiable Information.

4.3.2 Model Abuse

Many modern NLP techniques utilize some neural component, often in combination with embedding representations. In some of these cases, users interact with the models dynamically. Two broad categories of this interaction are: (1) centralized learning, in which users upload data to a centralized model for computations, and (2) decentralized (collaborative) learning, where computation is done locally with updates from a central server. If a malicious user has a point of access to either of these types of systems, information about the data can be inferred based on two ways (Ha et al., 2019): (1) black-box access, where the malicious user can query the model an unlimited number of times, and thus gain information from the model outputs, and (2) white-box access, where there is access to the original model parameters.

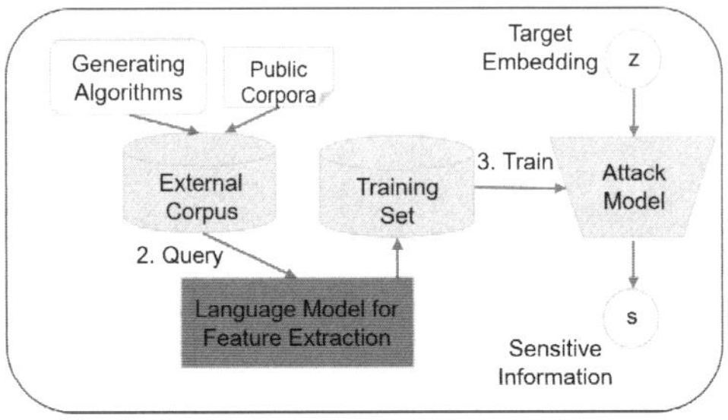

Figure 1: General Attack Pipeline, based on (Pan et al., 2020)

4.4 General Attack Pipeline

In order to define a general attack pipeline on NLP models as defined in both (Pan et al., 2020) and (Lyu et al., 2020), a few assumptions must be made about the attacker: (1) the attacker has access to the target text representations or model, (2) the attacker knows which pre-trained language model was used, and (3) the attacker is able to recreate the text representation. Note that these assumptions can be generalized to any target text representation, including plaintext. The assumptions enable the formulation of a general attack pipeline, illustrated in Figure 1. It enables an attacker in possession of sensitive text data encoded into some representation to *infer* the contents within. This idea of inference becomes the crucial basis to where Differential Privacy comes into play.

5 Differential Privacy in NLP

With the privacy issues that can arise when performing NLP tasks in mind, it is a logical step to consider the application of Differential Privacy to mitigate these privacy issues. Before one can consider *how* to do this, it may be be useful to understand *what* exactly Differential Privacy can protect against in the context of NLP.

5.1 Differential Privacy

Differential Privacy (Dwork, 2006) was first proposed with the goal of approaching privacy-preservation by protecting the *individual* in a database, and doing so with a mathematical guarantee. The underlying idea of *randomized response* is transferred to Differential Privacy by saying that the result of some query on two exactly identical databases except for one individual is similar within some threshold, defined by the privacy parameter ϵ, or the *privacy budget*. The exact foundations are covered briefly next, but one may refer to (Wood et al., 2018) for a thorough primer.

5.2 Foundations

The idea of Differential Privacy revolves around the protection of the individual in a database, or dataset. Traditionally, the "individual" being referred to corresponds to a single data entry, representing one individual's information structured according to the database's schema. With this in mind, the definition of Differential Privacy is expressed as the following inequality:

$$Pr[\mathcal{K}(D) \in S] \leq e^{\epsilon} Pr[\mathcal{K}(D') \in S] \quad (1)$$

The first important aspect to note in Equation 1 is that the output of some model is probabilistic, governed by some randomized function $\mathcal{K}$. Within this system, $\mathcal{K}$ has a possible set of outputs given an input database, denoted by S, where $S \subseteq Range(\mathcal{K})$. To make this concrete, given a database D as input to $\mathcal{K}$, S comprises of the values that can be returned as an output. Next, Eq. 1 refers to two *neighboring* databases D and D', which according to Differential Privacy, are two databases which differ in exactly one element, or more precisely one individual (*Hamming Distance* of 1). In effect, this means that any two databases which are identical minus one element are indeed *adjacent*, i.e. fit the description of D and D'. As a final component, Eq. 1 includes e^{ϵ} as a bound of how much the output of two adjacent datasets can differ, with ϵ as the *privacy parameter*. Intuitively, one can see that with a lower ϵ, the two outputs are constrained to be more similar, and on the flip side, a larger ϵ provides a bit more leeway. With this definition, the concept of *indistinguishably* is given form, with ϵ controlling how indistinguishable, or not, these operations on two neighboring databases must be. With a chosen ϵ, it is said that a function $\mathcal{K}$ achieves ϵ-differential privacy if Equation 1 is satisfied.

As one can see, this definition provides a quantifiable way to envision privacy in datasets, bolstered by a flexible privacy parameter. Translating this notion to the unstructured textual domain, though, comes with its challenges. Before these are discussed, one must first analyze how exactly Differential Privacy may be beneficial for privacy preservation in NLP, and in what way.

5.3 Protection *Against* Inferences?

Section 4 introduced some ways in which attackers can possibly gain sensitive information from text-based data, which revolve around the ability to *infer* information. When considering Differential Privacy as a potential defense for these attacks, it is important to notice that it does not protect against inferences themselves – and this applies to the application of Differential Privacy to any domain. In other words, a differentially private system is still vulnerable to inference attacks.

What Differential Privacy does offer, however, refers back to its core concept: protection of the *individual* against inferences. With NLP, that is with unstructured text data, this must be reasoned about differently. The application of Differential Privacy to the NLP domain would mean to provide the individuals (data contributors) plausible deniability as a protection against inference attacks. Put more concretely, one can take the example of keyword inference. Although an attacker still might be able to infer keywords from text representations, there would exist a level of uncertainty as to whether this extracted keyword actually represents the true, original keyword. As a result, the privacy protection given by Differential Privacy is rooted in this sense of plausible deniability, and not by a complete protection against inferences themselves.

5.4 The Challenge with Unstructured Data

Of course, the notion of the "individual" in a structured dataset is not immediately transferable to a non-structured dataset, such as a corpus of text (documents), yet this can be accomplished somewhat easily by reasoning about the individuals whose data is contained within such a corpus. With this thought, however, the concept of a "database" becomes unclear – is a database a collection of documents each tied to an individual, or is a database a single document comprised of many *individual words*? In the former case, applying Differential Privacy becomes difficult without a way to define adjacency beyond the traditional Hamming Distance. Likewise, the latter case would result in a very strict (and not practical) constraint.

The solution to applying standard Differential Privacy (i.e. in its original form) to NLP comes by converting text to a latent representation, and subsequently applying some differentially private mechanism. The biggest challenge, and seeming shortcoming, of such an approach is that using Differential Privacy in its original form imposes quite strict constraints in terms of how to perturb a given piece of text. Ultimately, this means that one must consider any two text documents to be adjacent, much like in the way that any two entries in a structured dataset are neighboring, thus taking a very conservative view of adjacency for text. A direct answer to this challenge comes with a generalized notion, introduced in Section 6.

5.5 Applications

Several implementations have appeared in the literature, all of which leverage Differential Privacy in the context of NLP tasks. As such, the following works represent the current thinking of how Differential Privacy can be used in practice for NLP.

In (Lyu et al., 2020), a method is proposed to perturb binary vector text representations in a simple, yet differentially private manner. (Weggenmann and Kerschbaum, 2018) focuses on TF-IDF vectors, leveraging the Exponential Mechanism (McSherry and Talwar, 2007) to create "synthetic" vectors. The authors in (Bo et al., 2019) add on an embedding reward system to encourage a diversity in the output text. (Beigi et al., 2019) also approach the utility vs. privacy problem with the introduction of a discriminator in a two-autoencoder setup.

In light of several works applying Differentially Private Stochastic Gradient Descent (DP-SGD) to address the memorization issue in deep neural NLP models (see Section 4.2), the authors in (Yu et al., 2021a) instead address privacy in the underlying language models. Here, differentially private fine-tuning is performed on several popular LMs.

Others focus on leveraging Differential Privacy in specific tasks, such as n-gram extraction (Kim et al., 2021), topic modeling (Vatsalan et al., 2021), or financial text classification (Basu et al., 2021a).

An interesting case comes with (Krishna et al., 2021), whose implementation is later refuted by the author of (Habernal, 2021). Similarly, Habernal (Habernal, 2022) claims that the DPText implementation of (Beigi et al., 2019) fails to be differentially private. This becomes the basis of an important discussion in Section 7.5.

6 Metric Differential Privacy for NLP

The idea of $d_{\mathcal{X}}$-privacy (Chatzikokolakis et al., 2013), also d-privacy or Metric Differential Privacy, was first introduced in 2013 as a generalization of Differential Privacy, with the goal of extending the concept beyond structured databases to arbitrary domains (e.g. location data). The key for achieving this comes with the reasoning about *adjacency* between two databases. In domains without an immediate notion of adjacency between individuals, it becomes necessary to find an alternate expression. The answer comes with the utilization of a (distance) metric existing within some *metric space*, whose members are often referred to as *points*. A relaxed sense of Differential Privacy thus enables its application to arbitrary domains endowed with a metric, and naturally this fits well with text.

6.1 Foundations

With an available metric, one can say that the distinguishability between two databases imposed by Differential Privacy depends on the distance between, or similarity of, these two databases. Therefore, the smaller the distance (and greater the similarity), the more similar (indistinguishable) the output of some function on the two databases must be. One can see that this is an extension of "differing by one individual" to "differing by some value". With this in mind, the original Equation 1 is adapted to fit this thinking, yielding:

$$Pr[\mathcal{K}(x) \in S] \leq e^{\epsilon d(x,x')} Pr[\mathcal{K}(x') \in S] \quad (2)$$

The implications of the new Equation 2 become clear: as the metric value between two inputs becomes larger (i.e. the inputs are less related), the distinguishability between the outputs resulting from them is allowed to be greater, and vice versa.

The task is now to apply the concepts of $d_{\mathcal{X}}$-privacy directly to NLP techniques utilizing text representations. It is important to note that there exist several other generalizations of Differential Privacy, as systematized in (Desfontaines and Pejó, 2019), yet the focus here is placed on $d_{\mathcal{X}}$-privacy due to its direct applicability to NLP tasks.

The main difference brought by the introduction of $d_{\mathcal{X}}$-privacy to NLP comes with the direct incorporation of a metric that "scales" the noise addition process to achieve Differential Privacy. In short: more similar meaning $\rightarrow$ more required indistinguishability. This new aspect comes as very convenient when dealing with text representations that already exist within spaces endowed with a distance (similarity) metric. $d_{\mathcal{X}}$-privacy allows for an increased flexibility in the sense that the underlying basis for a text representation (e.g. Euclidean vs. Hyperbolic) can change, without affecting the Differential Privacy inequality or compromising privacy preservation. This will prove to be useful as novel text representation methods are introduced.

6.2 Applications

Early approaches (Fernandes et al., 2018, 2019; Feyisetan et al., 2019a) involved working within the Euclidean space, i.e. using n-dimensional embeddings and the Laplace Mechanism. In (Feyisetan et al., 2019b), a shift to hyperbolic space was performed to model the hierarchical relationships within a language, leveraging them to perturb text. Finally, (Xu et al., 2020) makes the switch to the Mahalanobis (elliptical) norm which takes into account the shape of a particular space, resulting in better perturbation of sparse words. In a recent implementation (Carvalho et al., 2021), a bridge between Differential Privacy and Metric Differential Privacy is created through the use of a "Truncated Exponential Mechanism".

These works encapsulate the current thinking as to how $d_{\mathcal{X}}$-privacy can be implemented with the NLP models of today. One might imagine, however, that $d_{\mathcal{X}}$-privacy is not presently widely utilized due to its relative adolescence.

7 Discussion

With the application of Differential Privacy to the area of NLP also come several challenges. Ultimately, these limitations serve as a basis for future work and motivation for further improvements.

7.1 Utility

One would certainly be remiss to discuss the topic of Privacy-Enhancing Technologies without addressing the ever-present privacy-utility tradeoff. With this topic come many interesting findings from the literature, which are not necessarily all negative. With this said, the flip side of the coin presents an arguably more pressing discussion point. The usual effect is that as the ϵ parameter is set to be lower (stricter), the accuracy of a given task clearly decreases. Although this may be discouraging news, one must keep in mind that there is "no free lunch". The implications of this in terms of applying Differential Privacy to NLP, then, varies from case to case: one needs to decide to what degree privacy is necessary. I1 illustrates this complex decision in real-world applications by saying, "it's hard because yes your accuracy is lower if you use Differential Privacy, but if you don't use it you wouldn't get access to the data in the first place". The bright side comes from the flexibility that Differential Privacy offers. Adjusting ϵ enables one to experiment with the privacy and utility results of various parameters.

7.2 Benchmarking

Along with this current limitation of utility surfaces a clear lack in the present literature: benchmarking. The original works themselves and even dedicated papers such as (Basu et al., 2021b) often present findings regarding utility in the form of established scoring schemes (accuracy, F1). However, other important aspects of utility, especially in the mindset of NLP, are often ignored. Above all, the ability for these Differential Privacy implementations to produce coherent, grammatically correct language is often left out. One such paper, (Bo et al., 2019), does make this attempt, yet the results are not too convincing utility-wise. Therefore, a greater focus on syntactical and semantic coherence, sentence flow, and readability is needed.

Another aspect of benchmarking that is completely absent in the literature is the computational power, i.e. resources and time, required to implement the proposed methods. In order to make Differential Privacy for NLP a viable option going forward, more work on this will be required. Moreover, the question of transparency goes hand-in-hand with that of explainability, discussed in Section 7.5.

7.3 Structural Limitations

The key to reasoning about Differential Privacy in the unstructured domain of language comes with the important step of imposing a sort of "quasi-structure", e.g. by reasoning about text representations. This raises the question: is such a transfer of concepts always necessary when applying Differential Privacy? It was shown what happens when one attempts to deviate a bit from the rigorous definition put forth by Differential Privacy, specifically in the form of $d_{\mathcal{X}}$-privacy applying to arbitrary domains. Using $d_{\mathcal{X}}$-privacy as a case study, it becomes interesting to see how much one can diverge from the original sense of Differential Privacy to fit the needs of increasingly unstructured domains.

This becomes even more pertinent when addressing one of the major assumptions made throughout the literature, which is that the databases in question, whether structured or not, are *static* in nature. The notion that a database is static and does not evolve over time is indeed fitting with the original purpose and definition of Differential Privacy, yet it is less and less representative of a major part of the data being produced today (Kolajo et al., 2019). As a result, there now exists a discrepancy between the basis for proposed applications of Differential Privacy to NLP and what is used in state-of-the-art NLP. I3 states the problem more concretely:

> You have this beautiful theory, these nice robust proofs, all of the protection against side attacks and post-processing, compositionality, all of these lovely things... then you say something like you have an epsilon budget of 2 and it will be refreshed every 4 days, then the whole thing becomes meaningless at that point!

An investigation into this matter was started in (Cummings et al., 2018), and one more tailored to NLP surely needs to be conducted going forward.

Both with standard Differential Privacy and $d_{\mathcal{X}}$-privacy, the general approach so far in the literature is to (1) calculate some latent representation, (2) apply noise, and (3) proceed "downstream". The observed effect as shown in the literature has its flaws: the output after the noise addition often results in less than optimal language, with an overall lack of natural flow (also covered in Section 7.1).

Another current bottleneck that arises from these implications is the reliance on word embedding models. I3 calls this "the big elephant in the room". In earlier models where the corresponding embeddings are calculated based upon co-occurrence, the application of Differential Privacy makes more sense: perturbation results in semantically related noisy outputs. Recently, though, the utilization of contextual word embeddings (e.g. BERT) has become the prevalent method, and this presents a problem for the current thinking with Differential Privacy in NLP. With contextual embeddings, noise addition followed by a projection will result not in semantically similar words, but rather contextually similar ones – this is not desired for meaning- and utility-preserving private text representations. In essence, "with contextual embeddings, you would no longer be able to compute your nearest neighbor index, and [current Differential Privacy] becomes an impossibility" (I3).

7.4 Context

Beyond the problem posed by Differential Privacy with contextual text representations, the idea of *context* raises further questions. In the realm of textual data, the notion of what may be considered "private" presumably is quite dependent on the context in which this text was created or expressed, such as with customer reviews versus medical records. Even beyond this, the fact that *privacy* is an incredibly personal (and cultural) notion makes seemingly rigid definitions, such as that of Differential Privacy, hard to reason about. In this light, perhaps the idea of societal context must be investigated and incorporated in regards to text, so that differentially private NLP becomes more relevant. A related discussion built upon this idea follows in the ensuing section.

7.5 Explainability

Possibly one of the more crucial points that one must consider when applying Differential Privacy to NLP is the notion of explainability. The main question is: at what point is text truly private?

This question presents the biggest challenge to better explainability. At the core of the challenge lies the issue of *what exactly* it is about text that needs to become private. Of course, there could exist explicit words or phrases that contain sensitive information. Going deeper, though, one can also consider *stylometry* as a threat: our *writing style* is inherently personal. As pointed out by I1:

> The one thing with NLP that you won't get with a machine learning community is a deeper understanding of the language – what might be sensitive in the language, so things like an understanding of all the things you can learn from language – who is writing something, their profile – so having a more cohesive understanding of what is happening with text.

I2 also adds: "First thing we need to ask: is there really a privacy issue? What is the privacy issue? Can you demonstrate it?" With these questions in mind, the interesting aspect that comes with differentially private NLP is that the input text itself, or rather the text representations, are being perturbed, in contrast to operating on structured databases. This begs another question: how does perturbing word x and mapping it to word y increase the privacy protection of some individual? Another important design decision that seems to be ignored so far involves the so-called *selection problem*. In the literature, this issue is usually handled via the way in which text can be perturbed, or mapped, to other semantically similar text. The flip side of this coin, *selecting* what parts or sections of text are private and need to be handled accordingly, has received little to no recent attention. All of these questions are introduced when there is rarely a structured or direct mapping of database entries to individuals.

For a clearer answer, one can look to the crucial ϵ parameter. I4 supports this in saying, "We don't have a formal definition of privacy, but I think this mathematical guarantee has made it easier for us to work with privacy". This, however, turns out to be at the heart of the explainability issue. On one side, it allows for a relative quantification of privacy with respect to the value of the parameter. The challenging part is that this ϵ does not immediately lend itself to a clear path for explaining privacy in NLP. Even if this were possible, the literature seems to vary in terms of what ϵ makes sense for a given application of Differential Privacy to NLP, suggesting that the ϵ parameter might indeed just be relative to the task at hand. And as I2 formulates it, "the down side to [Differential Privacy] is that there is not a really strong operational interpretation of what privacy means". In this case, ϵ loses its global explainability value a bit, or rather, its "operational interpretation".

A final matter falling under the umbrella of explainability is the relative shroud of mystery surrounding Differential Privacy. Even amongst researchers, there seems to be a confusion of how to apply it correctly, as demonstrated by (Habernal, 2021) and (Habernal, 2022). As Habernal points out, the crux of the issue lies in the fact that "it seems non-trivial to get [Differential Privacy] right when applying it to NLP". The promise of Differential Privacy may be quite enticing, but as I1 puts it, "you have to get someone who understands the technology properly and understands the privacy-preserving nature". One can extrapolate from here and assume that explaining the mechanisms (and merits) of Differential Privacy to the general public will be a complex task. Accordingly, more emphasis on education and awareness should be afforded.

7.6 Future Directions: A Summary

The possibilities for future work relating to the application of Differential Privacy to NLP have been alluded to throughout and discussed via limitations in Section 7, but they are made explicit here:

- The **continued exploration of the privacy-utility tradeoff** when using Differential Privacy in NLP, as well as better explaining it.
- The **integration of Differential Privacy in more modern NLP architectures**, particularly sequence models, e.g. transformers.
- A focus on making Differential Privacy **compatible and usable with more recent text representations** (e.g. contextual embeddings and LLMs).
- The investigation of **Differential Privacy's role, applicability, and effectiveness in non-static data settings**: in particular, reasoning about how it could work with streaming (text) datasets.
- The topic of $d_{\mathcal{X}}$-privacy opens the doors to **other possible generalizations of Differential Privacy** tailored to NLP.
- Differential Privacy, NLP, and their **relation to regulation, policy, and implementation** in practice.
- **The ability to explain Differential Privacy** and its role in NLP, conducting research "in a way that people can understand" (I4).

8 Conclusion

The investigation into Differential Privacy's place within the NLP sphere results in many interesting findings and discussions. Understanding that there does indeed exist privacy vulnerabilities to NLP techniques, looking to Differential Privacy for a solution does not come without its challenges. Above all, this requires additional consideration as to how some core privacy concepts translate to the underlying structure (or lack thereof) powering current NLP tasks. The theoretical foundations and applications arising from recent literature have provided an excellent initial excursion into this topic, and from them, one can derive promising avenues for future improvements. Where Differential Privacy in NLP goes from here is yet to be seen, but the primary goal of this paper was to explore its foundations and to start the discussion on what this future might look like. Ultimately, the promise of applying Differential Privacy to mitigate privacy issues in NLP places it on the vanguard of Privacy-Enhancing Technologies, demanding further research.

Acknowledgements

This work has been supported by the German Federal Ministry of Education and Research (BMBF) Software Campus grant LACE 01IS17049 and the Bavarian Research Institute for Digital Transformation (bidt).

References

Martin Abadi, Andy Chu, Ian Goodfellow, H. Brendan McMahan, Ilya Mironov, Kunal Talwar, and Li Zhang. 2016. Deep learning with differential privacy. *Proceedings of the 2016 ACM SIGSAC Conference on Computer and Communications Security*.

Mohamed Abdalla, Moustafa Abdalla, Graeme Hirst, and Frank Rudzicz. 2020a. Exploring the privacy-preserving properties of word embeddings: Algorithmic validation study. *J Med Internet Res*, 22(7):e18055.

Mohamed Abdalla, Moustafa Abdalla, Frank Rudzicz, and Graeme Hirst. 2020b. Using word embeddings to improve the privacy of clinical notes. *Journal of the American Medical Informatics Association*, 27(6):901–907.

M. Al-Rubaie and J. M. Chang. 2019. Privacy-preserving machine learning: Threats and solutions. *IEEE Security Privacy*, 17(2):49–58.

Priyam Basu, Tiasa Singha Roy, Rakshit Naidu, and Zumrut Muftuoglu. 2021a. Privacy enabled financial text classification using differential privacy and federated learning.

Priyam Basu, Tiasa Singha Roy, Rakshit Naidu, Zümrüt Müftüoglu, Sahib Singh, and Fatemehsadat Mireshghallah. 2021b. Benchmarking differential privacy and federated learning for BERT models. *CoRR*, abs/2106.13973.

S. H. Begum and F. Nausheen. 2018. A comparative analysis of differential privacy vs other privacy mechanisms for big data. In *2018 2nd International Conference on Inventive Systems and Control (ICISC)*, pages 512–516.

Ghazaleh Beigi, Kai Shu, Ruocheng Guo, Suhang Wang, and Huan Liu. 2019. I am not what i write: Privacy preserving text representation learning.

Haohan Bo, Steven H. H. Ding, Benjamin C. M. Fung, and Farkhund Iqbal. 2019. Er-ae: Differentially-private text generation for authorship anonymization.

Amine Boulemtafes, Abdelouahid Derhab, and Yacine Challal. 2019. A review of privacy-preserving techniques for deep learning. *Neurocomputing*, 384.

Nicholas Carlini, Chang Liu, Úlfar Erlingsson, Jernej Kos, and Dawn Song. 2019. The secret sharer: Evaluating and testing unintended memorization in neural networks.

Nicholas Carlini, Florian Tramer, Eric Wallace, Matthew Jagielski, Ariel Herbert-Voss, Katherine Lee, Adam Roberts, Tom Brown, Dawn Song, Ulfar Erlingsson, Alina Oprea, and Colin Raffel. 2020. Extracting training data from large language models.

Ricardo Silva Carvalho, Theodore Vasiloudis, and Oluwaseyi Feyisetan. 2021. TEM: high utility metric differential privacy on text. *CoRR*, abs/2107.07928.

Kostas Chatzikokolakis, Miguel Andrés, Nicolás Bordenabe, and Catuscia Palamidessi. 2013. Broadening the scope of differential privacy using metrics.

Maximin Coavoux, Shashi Narayan, and Shay B. Cohen. 2018. Privacy-preserving neural representations of text.

Rachel Cummings, Sara Krehbiel, Kevin A. Lai, and Uthaipon Tantipongpipat. 2018. Differential privacy for growing databases. *CoRR*, abs/1803.06416.

Damien Desfontaines and Balázs Pejó. 2019. Sok: Differential privacies. *CoRR*, abs/1906.01337.

Cynthia Dwork. 2006. Differential privacy. In *33rd International Colloquium on Automata, Languages and Programming, part II (ICALP 2006)*, volume 4052 of *Lecture Notes in Computer Science*, pages 1–12. Springer Verlag.

Yanai Elazar and Yoav Goldberg. 2018. Adversarial removal of demographic attributes from text data. In *Proceedings of the 2018 Conference on Empirical Methods in Natural Language Processing*, pages 11–21, Brussels, Belgium. Association for Computational Linguistics.

Natasha Fernandes, Mark Dras, and Annabelle McIver. 2018. Author obfuscation using generalised differential privacy.

Natasha Fernandes, Mark Dras, and Annabelle McIver. 2019. Generalised differential privacy for text document processing.

Oluwaseyi Feyisetan, Borja Balle, Thomas Drake, and Tom Diethe. 2019a. Privacy- and utility-preserving textual analysis via calibrated multivariate perturbations.

Oluwaseyi Feyisetan, Tom Diethe, and Thomas Drake. 2019b. Leveraging hierarchical representations for preserving privacy and utility in text.

Max Friedrich, Arne Köhn, Gregor Wiedemann, and Chris Biemann. 2019. Adversarial learning of privacy-preserving text representations for de-identification of medical records. In *Proceedings of the 57th Annual Meeting of the Association for Computational Linguistics*, pages 5829–5839, Florence, Italy. Association for Computational Linguistics.

Vahid Garousi, Michael Felderer, and Mika V. Mäntylä. 2019. Guidelines for including grey literature and conducting multivocal literature reviews in software engineering. *Information and Software Technology*, 106:101 – 121.

T. Ha, T. K. Dang, T. T. Dang, T. A. Truong, and M. T. Nguyen. 2019. Differential privacy in deep learning: An overview. In *2019 International Conference on Advanced Computing and Applications (ACOMP)*, pages 97–102.

Ivan Habernal. 2021. When differential privacy meets NLP: The devil is in the detail. In *Proceedings of the 2021 Conference on Empirical Methods in Natural Language Processing*, pages 1522–1528, Online and Punta Cana, Dominican Republic. Association for Computational Linguistics.

Ivan Habernal. 2022. How reparametrization trick broke differentially-private text representation learning.

Khodor Hammoud, Salima Benbernou, Mourad Ouziri, Yücel Saygın, Rafiqul Haque, and Yehia Taher. 2019. Personal information privacy: what's next? CEUR Workshop Proceedings.

Zhanglong Ji, Zachary C. Lipton, and Charles Elkan. 2014. Differential privacy and machine learning: a survey and review.

W. Jiang, M. Murugesan, C. Clifton, and L. Si. 2009. t-plausibility: Semantic preserving text sanitization. In *2009 International Conference on Computational Science and Engineering*, volume 3, pages 68–75.

Kunho Kim, Sivakanth Gopi, Janardhan Kulkarni, and Sergey Yekhanin. 2021. Differentially private n-gram extraction.

Taiwo Kolajo, Olawande Daramola, and Ayodele Adebiyi. 2019. Big data stream analysis: a systematic literature review. *Journal of Big Data*, 6:47.

Moshe Koppel. 2002. Automatically categorizing written texts by author gender. *Literary and Linguistic Computing*, 17:401–412.

Satyapriya Krishna, Rahul Gupta, and Christophe Dupuy. 2021. Adept: Auto-encoder based differentially private text transformation. *CoRR*, abs/2102.01502.

N. Li, T. Li, and S. Venkatasubramanian. 2007. t-closeness: Privacy beyond k-anonymity and l-diversity. In *2007 IEEE 23rd International Conference on Data Engineering*, pages 106–115.

Xiao-Bai Li and Jialun Qin. 2018. Protecting privacy when releasing search results from medical document data. In *HICSS*.

Lingjuan Lyu, Xuanli He, and Yitong Li. 2020. Differentially private representation for nlp: Formal guarantee and an empirical study on privacy and fairness.

Ashwin Machanavajjhala, Daniel Kifer, Johannes Gehrke, and Muthuramakrishnan Venkitasubramaniam. 2007. L-diversity: Privacy beyond k-anonymity. *ACM Trans. Knowl. Discov. Data*, 1(1):3–es.

Frank McSherry and Kunal Talwar. 2007. Mechanism design via differential privacy. In *Annual IEEE Symposium on Foundations of Computer Science (FOCS)*. IEEE.

Xudong Pan, Mi Zhang, Shouling Ji, and Min Yang. 2020. Privacy risks of general-purpose language models. In *2020 IEEE Symposium on Security and Privacy (SP)*, pages 1314–1331.

Pierangela Samarati and Latanya Sweeney. 1998. Protecting privacy when disclosing information: k-anonymity and its enforcement through generalization and suppression.

Congzheng Song and Ananth Raghunathan. 2020. Information leakage in embedding models.

Aleena Thomas, David Ifeoluwa Adelani, Ali Davody, Aditya Mogadala, and Dietrich Klakow. 2020. Investigating the impact of pre-trained word embeddings on memorization in neural networks. In *Text, Speech, and Dialogue: 23rd International Conference, TSD 2020, Brno, Czech Republic, September 8–11, 2020, Proceedings*, page 273–281, Berlin, Heidelberg. Springer-Verlag.

Dinusha Vatsalan, Raghav Bhaskar, Aris Gkoulalas-Divanis, and Dimitrios Karapiperis. 2021. Privacy preserving text data encoding and topic modelling. In *2021 IEEE International Conference on Big Data (Big Data)*, pages 1308–1316.

Benjamin Weggenmann and Florian Kerschbaum. 2018. Syntf: Synthetic and differentially private term frequency vectors for privacy-preserving text mining.

Alexandra Wood, Micah Altman, Aaron Bembenek, Mark Bun, Marco Gaboardi, James Honaker, Kobbi Nissim, David O'Brien, Thomas Steinke, and Salil Vadhan. 2018. Differential privacy: A primer for a non-technical audience. *SSRN Electronic Journal*.

Zekun Xu, Abhinav Aggarwal, Oluwaseyi Feyisetan, and Nathanael Teissier. 2020. A differentially private text perturbation method using a regularized mahalanobis metric.

Da Yu, Saurabh Naik, Arturs Backurs, Sivakanth Gopi, Huseyin A. Inan, Gautam Kamath, Janardhan Kulkarni, Yin Tat Lee, Andre Manoel, Lukas Wutschitz, Sergey Yekhanin, and Huishuai Zhang. 2021a. Differentially private fine-tuning of language models. *CoRR*, abs/2110.06500.

Da Yu, Huishuai Zhang, Wei Chen, and Tie-Yan Liu. 2021b. Do not let privacy overbill utility: Gradient embedding perturbation for private learning. *CoRR*, abs/2102.12677.

*****Paper Not Available****

Proceedings of the Fourth Workshop on Privacy in Natural Language Processing, pages 12 - 12
July 15, 2022 ©2022 Association for Computational Linguistics

Privacy Leakage in Text Classification: A Data Extraction Approach

Adel Elmahdy*
University of Minnesota
adel@umn.edu

Huseyin A. Inan and **Robert Sim**
Microsoft Research
{huseyin.inan, rsim}@microsoft.com

Abstract

Recent work has demonstrated the successful extraction of training data from generative language models. However, it is not evident whether such extraction is feasible in text classification models since the training objective is to predict the class label as opposed to next-word prediction. This poses an interesting challenge and raises an important question regarding the privacy of training data in text classification settings. Therefore, we study the potential privacy leakage in the text classification domain by investigating the problem of unintended memorization of training data that is not pertinent to the learning task. We propose an algorithm to extract missing tokens of a partial text by exploiting the likelihood of the class label provided by the model. We test the effectiveness of our algorithm by inserting canaries into the training set and attempting to extract tokens in these canaries post-training. In our experiments, we demonstrate that successful extraction is possible to some extent. This can also be used as an auditing strategy to assess any potential unauthorized use of personal data without consent.

1 Introduction

Tremendous progress has recently been made in deep learning with natural language processing (NLP), which has led to significant advances in the model performance of a wide variety of NLP applications. The Transformer model (Vaswani et al., 2017; Wolf et al., 2020) has become the central and dominant architecture of many state-of-the-art NLP models. However, NLP models trained with personal data have also been shown to be vulnerable to fairness (Mehrabi et al., 2021) and privacy (Mireshghallah et al., 2020) issues, leading to adverse societal and ethical consequences.

One of the prime challenges of training machine learning models is the phenomenon of memorizing unique or rare training data. This may occur via what is called *unintended memorization* (Carlini et al., 2019) where the trained model memorizes out-of-distribution data in the training set that is irrelevant to the learning task. It is known that overfitting is not the cause of such a phenomenon, since the out-of-distribution data can be memorized as long as the model is still learning, making it challenging to mitigate through methods preventing overfitting such as early stopping. This phenomenon raises privacy concerns when the training set includes private data that may be inadvertently leaked, e.g., (Munroe, 2019).

The main focus of our work is to explore the memorization of training data in text classification models, which may contain private information collected from individuals. A motivating example in our study is a topic classification setting in which an individual can have private information, such as "I vote for X party" in the *politics* category, which can lead to a privacy violation if this information is leaked by the model.

We propose a data extraction algorithm to recover missing tokens of a partial text using the target model. The algorithm exploits the likelihood that the model generates for the target label of the text to infer the unknown tokens of the partial input text. To the best of our knowledge, this work is the first to demonstrate privacy leakage in a text classification setting by extracting tokens of canary sequences[1] via access to the underlying classification model. We conduct experiments to evaluate the performance of our extraction algorithm under

*This work was carried out as part of an internship at Microsoft Research (MSR), Redmond, WA. Adel Elmahdy is currently affiliated with the Department of Electrical and Computer Engineering and the Department of Computer Science and Engineering at the University of Minnesota.

[1] Canary sequences are out-of-distribution examples inserted into the training data. The trained model is then assessed to measure the degree to which the model has memorized such sequences.

Proceedings of the Fourth Workshop on Privacy in Natural Language Processing, pages 13 - 20
July 15, 2022 ©2022 Association for Computational Linguistics

a wide range of parameters such as the number of extracted tokens, the number of canary insertions, and the number of guesses for the extraction.

2 Background: Language Modeling

While this work is about text classification setting, it is built upon language models. In this section, we give a brief overview of langauge modeling. Language models are one of the pillars of state-of-the-art natural language processing pipelines. It has been well established that training these models at scale on large public corpora makes them adaptable to a wide range of downstream tasks (Bommasani et al., 2021).

Two widely used pre-training objectives are auto-regressive (AR) language modeling (Radford et al., 2018, 2019), and masked language modeling (MLM) (Devlin et al., 2019a; Liu et al., 2019). AR language modeling is based on modeling the probability distribution of a text corpus by decomposing it into conditional probabilities of each token given the previous context. Specifically, the distribution $\mathbb{P}(x_1, x_2, \ldots, x_n)$ of a sequence of tokens $(x_1, x_2, \ldots, x_n)$ can be factorized as $\mathbb{P}(x_1, x_2, \ldots, x_n) = \Pi_{i=1}^{n} \mathbb{P}(x_i | x_1, x_2, \ldots, x_{i-1})$ using the Bayes rule. A neural network is then trained to model each conditional distribution. We note that such a decomposition only captures the unidirectional context.

On the other hand, the MLM pre-training objective can utilize the bidirectional context since it is based on replacing a certain portion of tokens by a special symbol `[MASK]` and the model is trained to recover the original tokens at these corrupted positions. This bidirectional context information often carries useful signal on downstream language understanding tasks such as text classification tasks, leading to improved performance for models trained with MLM pre-training objective.

3 Related Work

The ultimate goal of training language models is to model the underlying distribution of a language, which should not require the memorization of training samples. However, recent results have shown that such memorization occurs in language models (Carlini et al., 2019; Zanella-Béguelin et al., 2020; Carlini et al., 2021; Inan et al., 2021; Mireshghallah et al., 2021; Carlini et al., 2022). In fact, when the data distribution is long-tailed, memorization might be necessary to achieve near-optimal accuracy on the test data (Feldman, 2020; Brown et al., 2021). Leakage of memorized content can cause privacy violations, especially in the case where the content can be linked to an individual (Art. 29 WP, 2014). There is a wide range of data leakage detection and prevention techniques for document classification in the literature, e.g., (Alneyadi et al., 2013; Katz et al., 2014; Alneyadi et al., 2015). However, several challenges and limitations are identified with these techniques (Alneyadi et al., 2016; Cheng et al., 2017).

In the case of language models trained with AR objective, the model learns to predict each and every next token given a sequence of tokens, which can theoretically lead to the leakage of the whole sequence if it is memorized by the model. (Carlini et al., 2021) has shown a successful extraction of memorized data, including various personal information from the GPT-2 model (Radford et al., 2019) belonging to this family.

For language models trained with MLM objective, the story has been different so far. For instance, (Lehman et al., 2021) shows that it is *not* easy to extract sensitive information from the BERT model (Devlin et al., 2019a) trained on private clinical data. This can be attributed to the fact that the MLM objective only targets a small portion of `[MASK]` tokens randomly replaced in the training set, as opposed to all the tokens in the AR setting.

Other forms of privacy leakage include membership inference, which has been widely explored in vision and text scenarios (Shokri et al., 2017; Yeom et al., 2018; Long et al., 2018; Truex et al., 2018; Song and Shmatikov, 2019; Nasr et al., 2019; Sablayrolles et al., 2019; Hayes et al., 2019; Salem et al., 2019; Leino and Fredrikson, 2020; Choquette-Choo et al., 2021; Shejwalkar et al., 2021), and property inference (Ganju et al., 2018; Zhang et al., 2021; Mahloujifar et al., 2022).

4 This Work: Text Classification

In this work, we turn our attention to the text classification setting, which spans a wide range of downstream applications (Minaee et al., 2021). Often times pre-training a language model is performed on large public datasets while fine-tuning requires a much smaller task-specific dataset whose privacy requirements might be much more strict. To the best of our knowledge, this setting has been largely unexplored and our goal is to understand potential privacy leakage in this setting.

In a text classification problem, the input is a sequence of tokens $\mathbf{x} = (x_1, x_2, \ldots, x_n)$ with a corresponding class label $y \in \{1, 2, \ldots, C\}$ where C is the number of classes. A model is trained to learn the relation between the input text and the corresponding class label. From a training data extraction perspective, the challenge of this setting is that here the goal is to maximize the log-likelihood of the correct class label (i.e. $\log \mathbb{P}(y|\mathbf{x})$), therefore, there is no language modeling involved among the tokens of the sequence $\mathbf{x}$. Although we cannot leverage the approaches introduced in prior work, it is also not clear a priori whether one can extract training data given the partial knowledge of the tokens and the label with query access to the model.

5 Threat Model and Testing Methodology

Similar to prior work (Shokri et al., 2017; Carlini et al., 2019), we assume black-box access to the target model, where it receives a sequence of tokens and outputs a class prediction with its corresponding likelihood. Our goal is to investigate whether it is possible to extract the remaining tokens given partial information about a sequence under this black-box access to the target model.

This framework encompasses both a malicious attacker who has partial information about personal data points and aims to fully reconstruct it by fiddling with the target model, and any individual who audits a target model to detect any unauthorized use of personal data (Song and Shmatikov, 2019) (or to check whether a model owner has actually complied with data deletion requests). We choose to focus on the latter case since it allows the data owner to inject "special" sequences into their data that would strongly indicate unauthorized use of personal data if a successful reconstruction is possible through the target model.

Similar to (Thakkar et al., 2021), we inject sequences of randomly selected tokens (with corresponding labels) into the training set. This mimics the existence of out-of-distribution data that is not pertinent to the learning process. We consider a testing procedure in which the goal of the extraction algorithm is to retrieve the last n tokens of a canary[2], where the sample space for each missing token is the entire tokenizer vocabulary. In the next section, we propose our extraction algorithm.

[2]Since the model is bidirectional, this could be any arbitrary n tokens in the sequence in general.

6 Proposed Extraction Algorithm

Given a partial sequence with missing tokens, the core idea of the proposed extraction algorithm is to choose the tokens such that the corresponding class label achieves the highest likelihood under the target model. Consider a canary sequence $\mathbf{x} = (x_1, x_2, \ldots, x_n)$ with a corresponding label y. Given a partial input, we iteratively query the underlying classification model to reconstruct the missing tokens. In particular, for a partial sequence $(x_1, x_2, \ldots, x_{t-1})$, the extraction algorithm enumerates all possible tokens from the vocabulary $\mathcal{V}$, evaluates the corresponding likelihood of the label y for each token by querying the classification model, and then returns the token that achieves the maximum likelihood. Formally, x_t is evaluated using the following optimization problem:

$$x_t = \arg\max_{v \in \mathcal{V}} \mathbb{P}\left(y | (x_1, x_2, \ldots, x_{t-1}, v)\right). \quad (1)$$

When a canary is repeated a few times in the training set, the extraction criterion in (1) may not yield a successful reconstruction of the canary sequence. In order to boost the performance of token extraction, we propose a data-dependent regularizer to penalize the tokens with the highest number of occurrences in the training set, counteracting the model's bias towards these tokens. Let $C(v)$ be the normalized number of occurrences of token v in the training data[3] for $v \in \mathcal{V}$. Consequently, the optimization problem with the regularized objective function is given by

$$x_t = \arg\max_{v \in \mathcal{V}} \mathbb{P}(y | (x_1, x_2, \ldots, x_{t-1}, v)) - \lambda \cdot C(v),$$

where λ is the regularization coefficient that controls the amount of penalization imposed on the tokens with frequent occurrences in the training data.

7 Experimental Evaluation

Dataset: We use the Reddit dataset[4]. We select the top 100 subreddits with largest number of reddit posts. We randomly sample 10000 and 2500 posts for the training and validation sets, respectively. The task is topic classification. In particular, given a user comment, the model is trained to predict the corresponding subreddit.

[3]This may be a strong requirement but approximations can be made via publicly available datasets. However, the extraction performance does not degrade much by setting $\lambda = 0$ (see Table 2 in Section 7).

[4]https://huggingface.co/datasets/reddit

	Original Canary		Supporting Canary	
	Subreddit	Repetitions	Subreddits	Repetitions
Table 2	Rarest	100	All Other Subreddits	1
Table 3	Rarest	Varying (1st Column)	All Other Subreddits	1
Table 4	Rarest	100	One Other Subreddit	Varying (1st Column)

Table 1: Information about the subreddits as well as numbers of repetitions of the original and supporting canaries for each experiment.

Model: We use the pre-trained BERT base model (Devlin et al., 2019b). We fine-tune the model for 10 epochs using AdamW optimizer (Loshchilov and Hutter, 2018) with weight decay 0.01, learning rate 1e-6, and batch size 32. We apply early stopping and take the snapshot that achieves the best validation performance to avoid overfitting. The average performance of the model over 10 runs with different random seeds is as follows:

- The average training accuracy is 47.69% for a training set size of 10k samples.
- The average validation accuracy is 42.94% for a validation set size of 2.5k samples.

Canary Construction: A canary sequence consists of a number of tokens and an associated class label. Each token in a canary is sampled uniformly at random from the BERT tokenizer vocabulary. We exclude subwords and sample from the remaining 17k whole words in the vocabulary. The reason for random sampling of tokens is to construct out-of-distribution posts with very high probability. For instance, an example of a randomly generated canary is "expected Disney activated Fulton rebel scalp Stark fraud myths Palestine." Finally, a canary sequence is inserted into the training set and repeated multiple times. This construction of canary sequences enables us to evaluate the model's unintended memorization of training data.

Intuitively, the most successful extraction is likely to occur within the rarest subreddit because there is more capacity for memorization. Hence, we insert a canary sequence of 10 randomly selected tokens into the rarest subreddit with 100 repetitions. This will be the original canary for which we would like to perform token extractions. Our first observation is that given the first 7 to 9

	Success Rate		
λ	Last Token	Last 2 Tokens	Last 3 Tokens
0	0.8	0.2	0
0.01	**0.9**	**0.3**	0
0.1	0.7	0.1	0
1	0.3	0.1	0
10	0.1	0	0

Table 2: Successful extraction rates of the proposed algorithm on the last 1 to 3 tokens for different values of the regularization parameter λ. The original canary is inserted 100 times in the rarest subreddit, while the supporting canary is inserted only once in all other subreddits. Random guess rate is only 0.0058 for the last token and 3.4e-5 for last 2 tokens.

tokens, the model is already confident in the corresponding label, and hence the missing token(s) do not exhibit themselves in our optimization. In particular, $\mathbb{P}\left(y|(x_1, x_2, \ldots, x_9, v)\right)$ has similar values for all $v \in \mathcal{V}$. Therefore, we inject one sequence into all other subreddits where the first 7 to 9 tokens are fixed, and the missing token(s) are chosen differently at random. These are called *supporting canaries* since they are not meant to be extracted, but enable the missing token(s) in the original canary to be crucial for maximizing the likelihood of the corresponding label, and hence the performance of the reconstruction is significantly boosted. Table 1 shows detailed information about the original and supporting canaries for each experiment whose results are presented next. The success of reconstruction is defined by the appearance of the missing token(s) in the top-k generation of the algorithm for a beam size k. Note that each experiment is run 10 times and the average success rate is reported. In Table 2, we present the results of the aforementioned experiment with $k = 100$. It is evident that the proposed algorithm achieves significant success rates for the extraction of a few tokens. However, it fails to reconstruct beyond more than two tokens since the search space becomes exponentially larger.

Table 3 presents the extraction results for the last token for various repetitions of the original canary and beam sizes. The supporting canary is inserted only once in all subreddits except the rarest. Although high repetition improves the success rate of our algorithm, which aligns well with the findings that memorization is exacerbated by duplication of a sequence (Kandpal et al., 2022; Carlini et al., 2022), low repetition still resurfaces the missing

Original Canary		Success Rate	
Repetitions	Beam Size	Our Algo.	Random Guess
100	50	**0.7**	0.0029
50	50	**0.5**	0.0029
25	50	**0.1**	0.0029
10	50	0	**0.0029**
100	100	**0.9**	0.0058
50	100	**0.5**	0.0058
25	100	**0.3**	0.0058
10	100	**0.1**	0.0058
100	200	**1**	0.0117
50	200	**0.9**	0.0117
25	200	**0.4**	0.0117
10	200	**0.2**	0.0117

Table 3: Successful extraction rates of the proposed algorithm compared to random guessing on the last token for various repetitions of the original canary and beam sizes. The supporting canary is inserted only once in all subreddits except the rarest. We set $\lambda = 0.01$.

Supporting Canary		Success Rate	
Repetitions	Beam Size	Our Algo.	Random Guess
99	50	**0.5**	0.0029
99	100	**0.5**	0.0058
99	200	**0.5**	0.0117
50	50	**0.4**	0.0029
50	100	**0.4**	0.0058
50	200	**0.5**	0.0117
25	50	**0.4**	0.0029
25	100	**0.5**	0.0058
25	200	**0.5**	0.0117
0	50	**0.1**	0.0029
0	100	**0.1**	0.0058
0	200	**0.1**	0.0117

Table 4: Success rates of extracting the last token under the proposed algorithm and random guess for various repetitions of the supporting canary and beam sizes. The original canary is inserted 100 times in the rarest subreddit. We set $\lambda = 0$.

token if the algorithm generates a larger number of candidates (i.e., larger beam size).

Instead of inserting one supporting canary into all subreddits except the rarest, we next investigate the insertion of a supporting canary into only one other arbitrarily chosen subreddit. Here we fix 100 repetitions of the original canary in the rarest subreddit and vary the repetition of the supporting canary in a different subreddit. Table 4 shows the extraction results for this experiment for various repetitions of the supporting canary and beam sizes. We can see that extraction is possible even when a canary is inserted into the rarest subreddit only, as shown in the last part of Table 4. However, the success rate improves greatly when we inject a supporting canary into another subreddit. The repetition we use for the subreddit does not seem to have an effect on the success rate of the extraction of the original canary.

8 Conclusion and Future Work

In this work, we studied the problem of unintentional memorization in a text classification setting. We developed an algorithm to extract unknown tokens of a partial text via access to the underlying classification model. Through experimental studies, we demonstrated the efficacy of the proposed extraction algorithm over random guessing.

Our experimental setting provides preliminary results and is subject to further exploration in future work. In particular, we injected the original canary into the rarest subreddit. In general, it would be interesting to range from the rarest to the most popular subreddit. We also used random tokens for canary construction, and it is of importance to extend it to more organic canaries. Finally, we leave investigating the effect of formal privacy guarantees, such as differentially private model training (Abadi et al., 2016), to future work.

9 Ethical Impact

This work explores the privacy implications of a text classification setting in which training is performed on sensitive and private data. We investigate whether data leakage is feasible under this setting. We believe that this work is a first step in determining the susceptibility of the underlying text classification model to privacy leakage and detecting unauthorized use of personal data. Both the dataset and the model are publicly available.

Acknowledgements

We thank members of Microsoft's Privacy in AI (PAI) research group for the valuable feedback in the early stages of this work. Special thanks to Fatemehsadat Mireshghallah for the insightful discussions, and Mashaal Musleh for the support in setting up the experiment environment. Finally, we thank the anonymous reviewers for their helpful comments toward improving the paper.

References

Martin Abadi, Andy Chu, Ian Goodfellow, H Brendan McMahan, Ilya Mironov, Kunal Talwar, and Li Zhang. 2016. Deep learning with differential privacy. In *Proceedings of the 2016 ACM SIGSAC conference on computer and communications security*, pages 308–318.

Sultan Alneyadi, Elankayer Sithirasenan, and Vallipuram Muthukkumarasamy. 2013. Adaptable N-gram classification model for data leakage prevention. In *7th International Conference on Signal Processing and Communication Systems (ICSPCS)*.

Sultan Alneyadi, Elankayer Sithirasenan, and Vallipuram Muthukkumarasamy. 2015. Detecting data semantic: a data leakage prevention approach. In *IEEE Trustcom/BigDataSE/ISPA*, volume 1, pages 910–917.

Sultan Alneyadi, Elankayer Sithirasenan, and Vallipuram Muthukkumarasamy. 2016. A survey on data leakage prevention systems. *Journal of Network and Computer Applications*, 62:137–152.

Art. 29 WP. 2014. Opinion 05/2014 on "Anonymisation Techniques".

Rishi Bommasani, Drew A Hudson, Ehsan Adeli, Russ Altman, Simran Arora, Sydney von Arx, Michael S Bernstein, Jeannette Bohg, Antoine Bosselut, Emma Brunskill, et al. 2021. On the opportunities and risks of foundation models. *arXiv preprint arXiv:2108.07258*.

Gavin Brown, Mark Bun, Vitaly Feldman, Adam Smith, and Kunal Talwar. 2021. When is memorization of irrelevant training data necessary for high-accuracy learning? In *Proceedings of the 53rd Annual ACM SIGACT Symposium on Theory of Computing*, pages 123–132.

Nicholas Carlini, Daphne Ippolito, Matthew Jagielski, Katherine Lee, Florian Tramer, and Chiyuan Zhang. 2022. Quantifying memorization across neural language models. *arXiv preprint arxiv.2202.07646*.

Nicholas Carlini, Chang Liu, Úlfar Erlingsson, Jernej Kos, and Dawn Song. 2019. The secret sharer: Evaluating and testing unintended memorization in neural networks. In *28th USENIX Security Symposium (USENIX Security 19)*, pages 267–284.

Nicholas Carlini, Florian Tramèr, Eric Wallace, Matthew Jagielski, Ariel Herbert-Voss, Katherine Lee, Adam Roberts, Tom Brown, Dawn Song, Úlfar Erlingsson, Alina Oprea, and Colin Raffel. 2021. Extracting training data from large language models. In *30th USENIX Security Symposium (USENIX Security 21)*, pages 2633–2650.

Long Cheng, Fang Liu, and Danfeng Yao. 2017. Enterprise data breach: causes, challenges, prevention, and future directions. *Wiley Interdisciplinary Reviews: Data Mining and Knowledge Discovery*, 7(5):e1211.

Christopher A. Choquette-Choo, Florian Tramer, Nicholas Carlini, and Nicolas Papernot. 2021. Label-only membership inference attacks. In *International Conference on Machine Learning*.

Jacob Devlin, Ming-Wei Chang, Kenton Lee, and Kristina Toutanova. 2019a. BERT: Pre-training of deep bidirectional transformers for language understanding. In *Proceedings of the 2019 Conference of the North American Chapter of the Association for Computational Linguistics: Human Language Technologies, Volume 1 (Long and Short Papers)*, NAACL-HLT '19, pages 4171–4186.

Jacob Devlin, Ming-Wei Chang, Kenton Lee, and Kristina Toutanova. 2019b. Bert: Pre-training of deep bidirectional transformers for language understanding. In *Proceedings of the Conference of the North American Chapter of the Association for Computational Linguistics: Human Language Technologies (NAACL-HLT)*, pages 4171–4186.

Vitaly Feldman. 2020. Does learning require memorization? A short tale about a long tail. In *Proceedings of the 52nd Annual ACM SIGACT Symposium on Theory of Computing*, STOC 2020, page 954–959.

Karan Ganju, Qi Wang, Wei Yang, Carl A. Gunter, and Nikita Borisov. 2018. Property inference attacks on fully connected neural networks using permutation invariant representations. In *Proceedings of the 2018 ACM SIGSAC Conference on Computer and Communications Security*, CCS '18, page 619–633. Association for Computing Machinery.

Jamie Hayes, Luca Melis, George Danezis, and Emiliano De Cristofaro. 2019. LOGAN: Membership inference attacks against generative models. In *Proceedings on Privacy Enhancing Technologies (PoPETs)*, volume 2019, pages 133–152.

Huseyin A Inan, Osman Ramadan, Lukas Wutschitz, Daniel Jones, Victor Rühle, James Withers, and Robert Sim. 2021. Training data leakage analysis in language models. *arXiv preprint arXiv:2101.05405*.

Nikhil Kandpal, Eric Wallace, and Colin Raffel. 2022. Deduplicating training data mitigates privacy risks in language models. *arXiv preprint arXiv:2202.06539*.

Gilad Katz, Yuval Elovici, and Bracha Shapira. 2014. Coban: A context based model for data leakage prevention. *Information sciences*, 262:137–158.

Eric Lehman, Sarthak Jain, Karl Pichotta, Yoav Goldberg, and Byron C Wallace. 2021. Does bert pretrained on clinical notes reveal sensitive data? In *Proceedings of the 2021 Conference of the North American Chapter of the Association for Computational Linguistics: Human Language Technologies*, pages 946–959.

Klas Leino and Matt Fredrikson. 2020. Stolen Memories: Leveraging model memorization for calibrated white-box membership inference. In *29th USENIX Security Symposium (USENIX Security 20)*, pages 1605–1622.

Yinhan Liu, Myle Ott, Naman Goyal, Jingfei Du, Mandar Joshi, Danqi Chen, Omer Levy, Mike Lewis, Luke Zettlemoyer, and Veselin Stoyanov. 2019. RoBERTa: A robustly optimized bert pretraining approach. *arXiv preprint arXiv:1907.11692*.

Yunhui Long, Vincent Bindschaedler, Lei Wang, Diyue Bu, Xiaofeng Wang, Haixu Tang, Carl A Gunter, and Kai Chen. 2018. Understanding membership inferences on well-generalized learning models. *arXiv preprint arXiv:1802.04889*.

Ilya Loshchilov and Frank Hutter. 2018. Decoupled weight decay regularization. In *International Conference on Learning Representations (ICLR)*.

Saeed Mahloujifar, Esha Ghosh, and Melissa Chase. 2022. Property inference from poisoning. In *IEEE Symposium on Security and Privacy (SP)*, pages 1569–1586.

Ninareh Mehrabi, Fred Morstatter, Nripsuta Saxena, Kristina Lerman, and Aram Galstyan. 2021. A survey on bias and fairness in machine learning. *ACM Computing Surveys (CSUR)*, 54(6):1–35.

Shervin Minaee, Nal Kalchbrenner, Erik Cambria, Narjes Nikzad, Meysam Chenaghlu, and Jianfeng Gao. 2021. Deep learning based text classification: A comprehensive review. *ACM Computing Surveys (CSUR)*, 54(3):1–40.

Fatemehsadat Mireshghallah, Huseyin Inan, Marcello Hasegawa, Victor Rühle, Taylor Berg-Kirkpatrick, and Robert Sim. 2021. Privacy regularization: Joint privacy-utility optimization in languagemodels. In *Proceedings of the 2021 Conference of the North American Chapter of the Association for Computational Linguistics: Human Language Technologies*, pages 3799–3807.

Fatemehsadat Mireshghallah, Mohammadkazem Taram, Praneeth Vepakomma, Abhishek Singh, Ramesh Raskar, and Hadi Esmaeilzadeh. 2020. Privacy in deep learning: A survey. *arXiv preprint arXiv:2004.12254*.

Randall Munroe. 2019. xkcd: Predictive models. `https://xkcd.com/2169`.

Milad Nasr, Reza Shokri, and Amir Houmansadr. 2019. Comprehensive privacy analysis of deep learning: Passive and active white-box inference attacks against centralized and federated learning. In *IEEE Symposium on Security and Privacy (SP)*, pages 739–753.

Alec Radford, Karthik Narasimhan, Tim Salimans, and Ilya Sutskever. 2018. Improving language understanding by generative pre-training.

Alec Radford, Jeffrey Wu, Rewon Child, David Luan, Dario Amodei, and Ilya Sutskever. 2019. Language models are unsupervised multitask learners.

Alexandre Sablayrolles, Matthijs Douze, Cordelia Schmid, Yann Ollivier, and Hervé Jégou. 2019. White-box vs black-box: Bayes optimal strategies for membership inference. In *Proceedings of the 36th International Conference on Machine Learning*, pages 5558–5567.

Ahmed Salem, Yang Zhang, Mathias Humbert, Mario Fritz, and Michael Backes. 2019. ML-Leaks: Model and data independent membership inference attacks and defenses on machine learning models. In *Network and Distributed Systems Security Symposium*.

Virat Shejwalkar, Huseyin A Inan, Amir Houmansadr, and Robert Sim. 2021. Membership inference attacks against NLP classification models. In *NeurIPS 2021 Workshop Privacy in Machine Learning*.

Reza Shokri, Marco Stronati, Congzheng Song, and Vitaly Shmatikov. 2017. Membership inference attacks against machine learning models. In *IEEE Symposium on Security and Privacy (SP)*, pages 3–18.

Congzheng Song and Vitaly Shmatikov. 2019. Auditing data provenance in text-generation models. In *Proceedings of the 25th ACM SIGKDD International Conference on Knowledge Discovery & Data Mining*, pages 196–206.

Om Dipakbhai Thakkar, Swaroop Ramaswamy, Rajiv Mathews, and Francoise Beaufays. 2021. Understanding unintended memorization in language models under federated learning. In *Proceedings of the Third Workshop on Privacy in Natural Language Processing*. Association for Computational Linguistics.

Stacey Truex, Ling Liu, Mehmet Emre Gursoy, Lei Yu, and Wenqi Wei. 2018. Towards demystifying membership inference attacks. *arXiv preprint arXiv:1807.09173*.

Ashish Vaswani, Noam Shazeer, Niki Parmar, Jakob Uszkoreit, Llion Jones, Aidan N Gomez, Łukasz Kaiser, and Illia Polosukhin. 2017. Attention is all you need. *Advances in Neural Information Processing Systems (NeurIPS)*, 30.

Thomas Wolf, Lysandre Debut, Victor Sanh, Julien Chaumond, Clement Delangue, Anthony Moi, Pierric Cistac, Tim Rault, Rémi Louf, Morgan Funtowicz, et al. 2020. Transformers: State-of-the-art natural language processing. In *Proceedings of the Conference on Empirical Methods in Natural Language Processing (EMNLP): System Demonstrations*, pages 38–45.

Samuel Yeom, Irene Giacomelli, Matt Fredrikson, and Somesh Jha. 2018. Privacy risk in machine learning: Analyzing the connection to overfitting. In *IEEE 31st Computer Security Foundations Symposium (CSF)*, pages 268–282.

Santiago Zanella-Béguelin, Lukas Wutschitz, Shruti Tople, Victor Rühle, Andrew Paverd, Olga Ohrimenko, Boris Köpf, and Marc Brockschmidt. 2020. Analyzing information leakage of updates to natural language models. In *Proceedings of the 2020 ACM SIGSAC Conference on Computer and Communications Security*, page 363–375.

Wanrong Zhang, Shruti Tople, and Olga Ohrimenko. 2021. Leakage of dataset properties in Multi-Party machine learning. In *30th USENIX Security Symposium (USENIX Security 21)*, pages 2687–2704.

Google Research

Training Text-to-Text Transformers with Privacy Guarantees

Natalia Ponomareva, Jasmijn Bastings, Sergei Vassilvitskii
{nponomareva, bastings, sergeiv}@google.com

Introduction

LMs are growing in size of data and parameters

Modern Transformer-based Large Language Models (LLMs) like T5, GPTs, etc.

- Are pre-trained on large amounts of data
- Can have up to billions of parameters
- Often released as modifiable checkpoints that can be easily fine-tuned to your task given limited amount of data
- Extremely good at various NLP tasks

Pre-training data is not really "public"

It still likely contains private information (e.g. data erroneously released to the web, copyrighted text, etc.)

- LLMs often exhibit episodic memory (e.g. **memorizing the training data** and outputting it verbatim) [1]. Preserved even after fine-tuning!
- Embeddings can also contain private data [3]
- This can expose owners of pre-trained and fine-tuned models to legal risks
- And could also be bad for generalization

Differential Privacy (DP) to the rescue

- DP [2] provides robust theoretical guarantees on information leakage
- DP can potentially fix some of the "empirical" privacy concerns like training data extraction attacks (memorization)

TL;DR
We investigate how DP-pretraining of T5 affects:

- Final task performance
- Robustness of models to "empirical" privacy concerns like memorization

Methods

Fully Private T5

The pre-training data is used twice: for the subword vocabulary and for gradient updates.

We modify both parts of T5:

- **Private SentencePiece**: a modification of SentencePiece that adds noise to histogram of word counts (works for any SP algorithm)
- **Private Training**: Modified optimization using DP Adam [4]

- Different from typical training, with DP we compute the loss and gradient **per individual example**
- We leverage JAX and its **vmap** operator which results in an acceptable compute time (**only 25%** slower than no DP-training)

Results

Does private (pre-) training hurt performance?

- We look at both private tokenization and private training separately, as well as their combination
- The private tokenizer serves as a **regularizer** on the pre-training task, improving pre-training acc.
- While private training results in a pre-training performance drop, *fine-tuning is hardly affected*
- Fully private model (private tokenizer+training) is even able to recover/improve pre-train accuracy but is not significantly better on fine-tuning tasks
- For some tasks fine-tuning performance can be better than that of a (non-private) baseline

Does private training prevent memorization?

- The way pre-training objective is formulated matters!
  - Span corruption is extremely robust to a (common definition of) memorization.
  - Prefix training exhibits a lot of memorization (the baseline outputs ~2% training data verbatim)
- Fully private models are able to mitigate the effect of memorization on commonly seen data:
  - for an ε of 6.23, Full DP-T5 models exhibit 366x less memorization
  - even very large values of ε like 320 provide 15x improvement in memorization.
- For rare training instances +/- **any** level of DP provides almost full elimination of memorization

Ablation

- Private *Training* has the most (positive) effect on memorization
- Private Tokenizer does affect memorization, albeit much less than private training.
- While private models do significantly reduce memorization, they do not fully eliminate it, especially for non-rare instances.

Conclusion

Summary

- DP is a theoretically justified way of providing privacy guarantees for pretraining Large Language Models
- Using T5, a Transformer-based encoder-decoder, we investigated whether differential privacy (DP) would hurt utility (i.e., pre-training accuracy) and subsequent fine-tuning performance
- Fully private pre-training of Large Language Models can preserve good pre-training performance
- Can achieve comparable final task (fine-tuning) performance
- Can also mitigate empirical privacy attacks like training data extraction
- Private training is only 25% slower than training a baseline without DP.
- It can be implemented efficiently using JAX's vmap operator.
- Code: bit.ly/private_text_transformers

Author Index